proverbs
for
people

illustrated

Vern
McLellan

Nate Owens, Illustrator

HARVEST HOUSE PUBLISHERS
EUGENE, OREGON

Dedicated To

My wife, Mary, and our children,
Lorie, Jack, Kent, Bonnie, Lucinda, & Kenya Beth
who patiently, lovingly, and smilingly cheered me
through this project.

Scriptures are taken from THE LIVING BIBLE, Copyright
© 1971, Tyndale House Publishers, Wheaton, Illinois. Used
by permission.

PROVERBS FOR PEOPLE

Copyright © 1983 by Harvest House Publishers
Eugene, Oregon 97402

Library of Congress Catalog Card Number 82-83841
ISBN 0-89081-326-4

Printed in the United States of America.

Introduction

The practice of using proverbs has often been credited to the famous philosopher Aristotle who is claimed to be the first person to have put together a collection of proverbs. However, the Bible preceded him with its extraordinary Book of Proverbs—timely and timeless gems of wit, wisdom, and insight.

Exactly what is a proverb? Here are some of the best definitions I've encountered:

> "A homespun teaching on an everyday issue."
> "A small statement teaching enormous truth."
> "An electrifying flash of perception."
> "The wit of one and the wisdom of many."
> "A flash of light into a dark, unknown place."

Do proverbs have an impact? For more than 20 years, I've watched audiences of all ages respond to these pointed, pithy, pungent, powerful proverbs. Appearances in schools, conferences, conventions, churches, and civic groups have impressed me with the fact that people are looking for handles with which to get a grip on truth that will help them face the challenges, crises, and opportunities of life.

Proverbs cross over international borders. Many of the proverbs on the following pages have come from Asia, Europe, the Middle East, and Australia. Others appeared anonymously in newspapers, magazines, church bulletins, or on billboards, restaurant place mats or truck doors.

I've tried to match the wisdom of Solomon or the counsel of the psalmist with this potpourri of proverbs. I believe you will find distilled wisdom and sometimes humorous insight that can be applied to all dimensions of living in these demanding times.

—*Vern McLellan*

He who holds his tongue rarely has trouble holding his friends...

MUM

Proverbs 18:19

It is harder to win back the friendship of an offended brother than to capture a fortified city. His anger shuts you out like iron bars.

5

He who drives a school bus gets an education in a hurry...

Proverbs 9:9

Teach a wise man, and he will be the wiser; teach a good man, and he will learn more.

He who is afraid of the past may have reason to be afraid of his future...

Proverbs 26:13-14

The lazy man won't go out and work. "There might be a lion outside!" he says. He sticks to his bed like a door to its hinges.

He who jumps at conclusions cannot always expect a happy landing...

Proverbs 18:13, 17

What a shame—yes, how stupid!—to decide before knowing the facts! Any story sounds true until someone tells the other side and sets the record straight.

The best safe for a man's money is a prudent wife...

Proverbs 18:22

The man who finds a wife finds a good thing; she is a blessing to him from the Lord.

He who fears God has nothing else to fear...

Proverbs 1:7

How does a man become wise? The first step is to trust and reverence the Lord!

He who stands for nothing will fall for anything...

Proverbs 4:7

Determination to be wise is the first step toward becoming wise! And with your wisdom, develop common sense and good judgment.

He who has no battles will have no victories...

Proverbs 21:31

Go ahead and prepare for the conflict, but victory comes from God.

He who parades his virtues seldom leads the parade...

Proverbs 3:7-8

Don't be conceited, sure of your own wisdom. Instead trust and reverence the Lord, and turn your back on evil; when you do that, then you will be given renewed health and vitality.

13

He who finds his son on the wrong track should provide switching facilities...

Proverbs 23:13

Don't fail to correct your children; discipline won't hurt them.

He who worries pays interest on trouble before it is due...

Psalm 37:8

Stop your anger! Turn off your wrath. Don't fret or worry—it only leads to harm.

He who is never criticized is not breathing...

Proverbs 15:31-32

If you profit from constructive criticism you will be elected to the wise men's hall of fame. But to reject criticism is to harm yourself and your own best interests.

She who broods over her troubles will have a perfect hatch...

Proverbs 8:17

He who seeks, finds.

He who overeats may live beyond his seams...

Proverbs 23:19-20

O my son, be wise and stay in God's paths; don't carouse with drunkards and gluttons, for they are on their way to poverty.

18

He who is a stranger to prayer is a stranger to power...

Proverbs 15:29

The Lord is far from the wicked, but he hears the prayers of the righteous.

He who lives only for *himself runs a very small business...*

Proverbs 11:24-25

It is possible to give away and become richer! It is also possible to hold on too tightly and lose everything. Yes, the liberal man shall be rich! By watering others, he waters himself.

20

He who thinks he can find some big strawberries at the bottom of the box is an optimist...

Proverbs 15:15

When a man is gloomy, everything seems to go wrong; when he is cheerful, everything seems right!

He who battles his way to the top, too often bottles his way to the bottom...

Proverbs 21:17

A man who loves pleasure becomes poor; wine and luxury are not the way to riches!

He who looks up to God rarely looks down on people...

Proverbs 22:4

True humility and respect for the Lord lead a man to riches, honor and long life.

He who aims at nothing is sure to hit it...

Proverbs 17:24

Wisdom is the main pursuit of sensible men, but a fool's goals are at the ends of the earth.

He who thinks by the inch and talks by the yard deserves to be kicked by the foot...

Proverbs 10:19-20

Don't talk so much. You keep putting your foot in your mouth. Be sensible and turn off the flow! When a good man speaks, he is worth listening to, but the words of the foolish are a dime a dozen.

He who keeps a cool head stays out of hot water...

Proverbs 16:32

It is better to be slow-tempered than famous;
it is better to have self-control than to control
an army.

He who knows everything has a lot to learn...

Proverbs 12:23

A wise man doesn't display his knowledge, but a fool displays his foolishness.

He who has a sharp tongue usually cuts his own throat...

Proverbs 12:18

Some people like to make cutting remarks, but the words of the wise soothe and heal.

He who fears the future is likely to fumble the present...

Proverbs 11:23

The good man can look forward to happiness, while the wicked can expect only wrath.

He who never makes a mistake works for the man who does...

Proverbs 28:13

A man who refuses to admit his mistakes can never be successful. But if he confesses and forsakes them, he gets another chance.

He who lacks courage thinks with his legs...

Proverbs 3:24-25

With wisdom and common sense on guard you can sleep without fear; you need not be afraid of disaster or the plots of wicked men, for the Lord is with you.

He who rolls up his sleeves seldom loses his shirt...

Proverbs 12:11

Hard work means prosperity; only a fool idles away his time.

He who growls all day lives a dog's life...

Proverbs 15:4

Gentle words cause life and health; griping brings discouragement.

He who abandons himself to God will never be abandoned by God...

Proverbs 16:33

We toss the coin, but it is the Lord who controls its decision.

He who stops at third base to congratulate himself will never score a home run...

Proverbs 27:2
Don't praise yourself; let others do it!

He who asks a question may be a fool for five minutes, but he who never asks a question remains a fool forever...

Proverbs 15:14

A wise man is hungry for truth, while the mocker feeds on trash.

He who takes cares to bed will sleep with a pack on his back...

Proverbs 16:3

Commit your work to the Lord, then it will succeed.

He who talks without thinking runs more risks than he who thinks without talking...

Proverbs 11:9
Evil words destroy. Godly skill rebuilds.

He who drives too fast into the next county may wind up in the next world...

Proverbs 21:16

The man who strays away from common sense will end up dead!

He who wants to be outstanding in his field must use horse sense...

PRESIDENT
HORSCENTS

Proverbs 24:13

My son, honey whets the appetite, and so does wisdom! When you enjoy becoming wise, there is hope for you! A bright future lies ahead!

He who wakes up and finds himself a success hasn't been asleep...

Proverbs 10:5

A wise youth makes hay while the sun shines, but what a shame to see a lad who sleeps away his hour of opportunity.

He who speaks much is much mistaken...

Ecclesiastes 5:2-3

Don't be a fool who doesn't even realize it is sinful to make rash promises to God...so let your words be few...being a fool makes you a blabber mouth.

He who fiddles around seldom gets to lead the orchestra...

Proverbs 14:23

Work brings a profit, talk brings poverty!

He who cannot stand the heat should stay out of the kitchen...

Proverbs 24:10

You are a poor specimen if you can't stand the pressure of adversity.

46

He who waits upon fortune is never sure of dinner...

LADY LUCK

LUCKY SHOE

WAITING FOR FORTUNE

CRYSTAL BALL

Proverbs 19:15

A lazy man sleeps soundly—and goes hungry!

He who makes the doctor his heir is a fool...

Proverbs 28:26

A man is a fool to trust himself! But those who use God's wisdom are safe.

48

He who won't be counseled can't be helped—
Benjamin Franklin...

Proverbs 13:10

Pride leads to arguments; be humble, take advice and become wise.

He who gossips usually winds up in his own mouth trap...

Proverbs 16:28

An evil man sows strife; gossip separates the best of friends.

He who is a good listener is a silent flatterer...

Proverbs 2:1

Every young man who listens to me and obeys my instructions will be given wisdom and good sense.

He who tunes up in the morning stays in harmony all day...

Psalm 5:3

Each morning I will look to you in heaven and lay my requests before you, praying earnestly.

52

He who thinks before he acts makes one step do the work of five...

Proverbs 13:16

A wise man thinks ahead; a fool doesn't, and even brags about it!

He who wants to make a fool of himself will always find plenty of help...

Proverbs 1:10,17

If young toughs tell you, "Come and join us"—turn your back on them! When a bird sees a trap being set, it stays away.

54

He who thinks too little usually talks too much...

Proverbs 15:28

A good man thinks before he speaks; the evil man pours out his evil words without a thought.

He who has money to burn eventually meets his match...

Proverbs 23:4-5

Don't weary yourself trying to get rich. Why waste your time? For riches can disappear as though they had the wings of a bird!

He who needs advice most usually likes it least...

Proverbs 12:15

A fool thinks he needs no advice, but a wise man listens to others.

He whose pants wear out before his shoes is making too many contacts at the wrong places...

Proverbs 20:4

If you won't plow in the cold, you won't eat at the harvest.

He who is too big for a small job is too small for a big one...

Proverbs 11:2

Proud men end in shame, but the meek become wise.

He who falls in love with himself will have no rivals...

Proverbs 16:18-19

Pride goes before destruction and haughtiness before a fall. Better poor and humble than proud and rich.

He who flies into a rage always makes a bad landing...

Proverbs 29:9

There's no use arguing with a fool. He only rages and scoffs, and tempers flare.

He who seeks trouble always finds it...

Proverbs 21:23

Keep your mouth closed and you'll stay out of trouble.

He who is old should give advice; he who is young should take it...

Proverbs 20:29

The glory of young men is their strength; of old men, their experience.

63

He who teaches the Bible is never a scholar; he is always a student...

Proverbs 1:5-6

I want those already wise to become wiser and become leaders by exploring the depths of learning in these nuggets of faith.

He who is always blowing a fuse is usually in the dark...

Proverbs 30:33

As the churning of cream yields butter, and a blow to the nose causes bleeding, so anger causes quarrels.

65

He whose conversation is wanting in depth often makes up for it in length...

Proverbs 17:27-28

The man of few words and settled mind is wise; therefore, even a fool is thought to be wise when he is silent. It pays him to keep his mouth shut.

66

He who stretches the truth won't make it last any longer...

Proverbs 12:19

Truth stands the test of time; lies are soon exposed.

He who helps someone up the hill gets closer to the top himself...

Ecclesiastes 9:10

Whatever you do, do well, for in death, where you are going, there is no working or planning, or knowing, or understanding.

He who wants to get into WHO'S WHO must first learn what's what...

Proverbs 1:8-9

Only fools refuse to be taught. Listen to your father and mother. What you learn from them will stand you in good stead; it will gain you many honors.

He who is at war with himself will also be at war with others...

Proverbs 25:28

A man without self-control is as defenseless as a city with broken-down walls.

He who does not grow, grows smaller...

Proverbs 4:1-2

Young men, listen to me as you would to your father. Listen, and grow wise, for I speak the truth—don't turn away.

He who is guilty runs when no one is chasing him...

Proverbs 28:1

The wicked flee when no one is chasing them!
But the godly are bold as lions.

He who persists in knocking will succeed in entering...

Proverbs 20:13

If you love sleep, you will end in poverty. Stay awake, work hard, and there will be plenty to eat.

He who does <u>not</u> *make a choice makes a choice...*

Isaiah 50:7

Because the Lord God helps me, I will not be dismayed; therefore, I have set my face like a flint to do his will, and I know that I will triumph.

He who can't control his temper is like a city without defenses...

Proverbs 22:24-25

Keep away from angry, short-tempered men, lest you learn to be like them and endanger your soul.

He who is aware of his folly is wise...

Proverbs 3:13-14

A man who knows right from wrong and has good judgment and common sense is happier than the man who is immensely rich.

He who has not tasted the bitter does not understand the sweet...

Proverbs 14:10

Only the person involved can know his own bitterness or joy—no one else can really share it.

He who brags what he's doing tomorrow was probably doing the same yesterday...

Proverbs 27:1

Don't brag about your plans for tomorrow—wait and see what happens.

He who tries to please everybody will die before his time...

Proverbs 16:7

When a man is trying to please God, God makes even his worst enemies to be at peace with him.

He who wasts today lamenting yesterday will waste tomorrow lamenting today...

Proverbs 29:25

Fear of man is a dangerous trap, but to trust in God means safety.

He whose hand gives, gathers...

Proverbs 25:21

If your enemy is hungry, give him food! If he is thirsty, give him something to drink! This will make him feel ashamed of himself, and God will reward you.

She *who sings her own praise is usually off key...*

Proverbs 11:22

A beautiful woman lacking discretion and modesty is like a fine gold ring in a pig's snout.

He who is not afraid to face the music may someday lead the band...

Proverbs 10:17

Anyone willing to be corrected is on the pathway to life. Anyone refusing has lost his chance.

He who only stands and cheers also performs an important service...

Joshua 22:5

Be sure to continue to obey all of the commandments Moses gave you. Love the Lord and follow his plan for your lives. Cling to him and serve him enthusiastically.

He who promises and gives nothing is comfort to a fool...

Ecclesiastes 5:4

So when you talk to God and vow to him that you will do something, don't delay in doing it, for God has no pleasure in fools.

He who answers speedily errs speedily...

Proverbs 19:11

A wise man restrains his anger and overlooks insults. This is to his credit.

He who is honest secretly welcomes a press agent...

Proverbs 11:1

The Lord hates cheating and delights in honesty.

He who pulls on the oars doesn't have time to rock the boat...

Proverbs 22:29

Do you know a hard-working man? He shall be successful and stand before kings!

He who is humble will not stumble...

Proverbs 3:34

The wise are promoted to honor, but fools are promoted to shame.

He who is a wise man by day is no fool by night...

NEW BATTERIES
FRESH BATTERIES

Proverbs 9:11-12

"I, wisdom, will make the hours of your day profitable and the years of your life more fruitful." Wisdom is its own reward, and if you scorn her, you hurt only yourself.

He who loafs never becomes a successful breadwinner...

CUPBOARD

BIG LOAF

Proverbs 13:4

Lazy people want much but get little, while the diligent are prospering.

He who drinks commits suicide on the installment plan...

Proverbs 20:1

Wine gives false courage, hard liquor leads to brawls; what fools men are to let it master them, making them reel drunkenly down the street.

92

He who will not economize may have to agonize...

Proverbs 21:20

The wise man saves for the future, but the foolish man spends whatever he gets.

He who fails to put first things first winds up second best...

Proverbs 1:7-8

How does a man become wise? The first step is to trust and reverence the Lord!

He who gazes at the stars is at the mercy of the puddles on the road...

Ecclesiastes 6:7

Wise men and fools alike spend their lives scratching for food, and never seem to get enough.

He who keeps a cool head avoids a hot argument...

Proverbs 15:18

A quick-tempered man starts fights; a cool-tempered man tries to stop them.

He who feeds his faith will starve his doubts to death...

Proverbs 3:4-5

If you want favor with both God and man, and a reputation for good judgment and common sense, then trust the Lord completely; don't ever trust yourself.

He who will not answer to the rudder must answer to the rocks...

Proverbs 22:3

A prudent man foresees the difficulties ahead and prepares for them; the simpleton goes blindly on and suffers the consequences.

He who toots his own horn the loudest is in the biggest fog...

Proverbs 26:12

There is one thing worse than a fool, and that is a man who is conceited.

He who sings frightens away his ills...

Proverbs 29:5-6

Flattery is a trap; evil men are caught in it but good men stay away and sing for joy.

He who expects nothing shall not be disappointed...

Proverbs 16:9

We should make plans—counting on God to direct us.

He who stares at the clock watches time pass...

Psalm 90:12

Teach us to number our days and recognize how few they are; help us to spend them as we should.

He who does not pray when the sun shines will not know how to pray when the clouds roll in...

Isaiah 55:6

Seek the Lord while you can find him. Call upon him now while he is near.

He who has a loose tongue may soon find himself in a tight place...

Proverbs 13:3

Self-control means controlling the tongue! A quick retort can ruin everything.

He who delivers the goods is never long out of a job...

Proverbs 19:8

He who loves wisdom loves his own best interest and will be a success.

He who wants to eat the kernel must first crack the nut...

Proverbs 16:24

Kind words are like honey—enjoyable and healthful.

He who depends on the breaks to win usually goes broke...

Proverbs 12:9

It is better to get your hands dirty—and eat—than to be too proud to work—and starve.

He who uses horse sense will live a stable life...

Proverbs 20:15

Good sense is far more valuable than gold or precious jewels.

He who wants to make a splash in the puddle of life must be willing to jump...

Deuteronomy 31:6

Be strong! Be courageous! Do not be afraid of them! For the Lord your God will be with you. He will neither fail you nor forsake you.

109

He who moves a mountain starts by carrying away small stones...

Exodus 14:15

Then the Lord said to Moses, "Quit praying and get the people moving! Forward, march!"

He who tells the truth need not remember what he said...

Proverbs 12:5

A good man's mind is filled with honest thoughts; an evil man's mind is crammed with lies.

111

He who cuts his own wood warms himself twice...

Proverbs 12:14

Telling the truth gives a man great satisfaction, and hard work returns many blessings to him.

He who loses his temper usually loses...

Proverbs 29:22

A hot-tempered man starts fights and gets into all kinds of trouble.

He who deals in sunshine does more business than he who peddles clouds...

Proverbs 13:12

Hope deferred makes the heart sick; but when dreams come true at last, there is life and joy.

He who crosses an ocean twice without taking a bath is a dirty double-crosser...

Psalm 26:4

When arguing with a rebel, don't use foolish arguments as he does, or you will become as foolish as he is!

He who carries chips on his shoulder has wood higher up...

Proverbs 17:17

He who walks in when others walk out is a true friend.

He who oversleeps cannot make dreams come true...

Ecclesiastes 5:7

Dreaming instead of doing is foolishness and there is ruin in a flood of empty words; fear God instead.

He who overeats breaks the feed limit...

Proverbs 23:1

When dining with a rich man, be on your guard and don't stuff yourself, though it all tastes so good.

He who occupies a place in the sun should expect blisters...

MY PEDESTAL

Proverbs 29:1

The man who is often reproved but refuses to accept criticism will suddenly be broken and never have another chance.

He who itches for success must be willing to scratch for it...

Psalm 37:5

Commit everything you do to the Lord. Trust Him to help you do it and He will.

He who keeps his mouth closed does not gather feet...

Proverbs 18:21

Those who love to talk will suffer the consequences. Men have died for saying the wrong thing.

He who cannot do something big can do something small in a big way...

SPESHUL TODAY ONLY

BIG SALE

2¢ REBAIT

FREE BALLOON

LEMONADE 5¢

LAST CHANCE

Proverbs 15:19

A lazy fellow has trouble all through life; the good man's path is easy!

He who kicks up a storm should expect rough sailing...

Proverbs 18:2

A rebel doesn't care about the facts. All he wants to do is yell.

123

He who takes the wrong road makes the journey twice...

Proverbs 22:6

Teach a child to choose the right path, and when he is older he will remain upon it.

He who wants to be a picture of health must be in a good frame of mind...

Proverbs 17:22

A cheerful heart does good like medicine, but a broken spirit makes one sick.

He who invented the eraser had the human race pretty well sized up...

MODERN MAN

Psalm 51:9-10

Don't keep looking at my sins—erase them from your sight. Create in me a new, clean heart, O God, filled with clean thoughts and right desires.

He who never picks up the dinner check has an impediment in his reach...

Proverbs 21:25-26

The lazy man longs for many things but his hands refuse to work. He is greedy to get, while the godly love to give!

He who is foolish in the fault, let him be wise to the punishment...

Proverbs 13:18

If you refuse criticism you will end in poverty and disgrace; if you accept criticism you are on the road to fame.

128

The wise man does not need to blush for changing his purposes...

THIS WAY

Proverbs 13:19

It is pleasant to see plans develop. That is why fools refuse to give them up even when they are wrong.

He who lives well preaches well...

Proverbs 4:8-10

If you exalt wisdom, she will exalt you. Hold her fast and she will lead you to great honor; she will place a beautiful crown upon your head.

He who preaches strife is the devil's chaplain...

Proverbs 26:21

A quarrelsome man starts fights as easily as a match sets fire to paper.

He who has begun his task has half done it...

STEP 1
WIDGET FIXER

Proverbs 24:27

Develop your business first before building your house.

The best way to save face is keep the lower part shut...

Ecclesiastes 5:5

It is far better not to say you'll do something, than to say you will and then not do it.

He who does not have a smiling face should not open his shop...

Proverbs 15:13

A happy face means a glad heart; a sad face means a breaking heart.

He who hears with wooden ears has block in between...

Proverbs 23:9

Don't waste your breath on a rebel. He will despise the wisest advice.

He who throws dirt loses ground...

Proverbs 10:14

A wise man holds his tongue. Only a fool blurts out everthing he knows; that only leads to sorrow and trouble.

He who gossips lets the chat out of the bag...

Proverbs 11:13

A gossip goes around spreading rumors, while a trustworthy man tries to quiet them.

He who trusts all things to chance makes a lottery of his life...

Psalm 20:7 KJV

Some trust in chariots, and some in horses; but we will remember the name of the Lord our God.

He who is flat on his back has no where to look but up...

Psalm 42:11

But O my soul, don't be discouraged. Don't be upset. Expect God to act! For I know that I shall again have plenty of reason to praise him for all he will do.

He who receives a good turn should never forget it; he who does one should never remember it...

Proverbs 11:17

Your own soul is nourished when you are kind; it is destroyed when you are cruel.

He who loses wealth loses much but he who loses courage loses all...

Proverbs 20:24

Since the Lord is directing our steps, why try to understand everything that happens along the way?

He who repeats the ill he hears of another is the true slanderer...

Proverbs 18:6-8

A fool gets into constant fights. His mouth is his undoing! His words endanger him. What dainty morsels rumors are. They are eaten with great relish!

142

He who beats his head against a wall of problems ends up a "sorehead"...

Proverbs 27:12

A sensible man watches for problems ahead and prepares to meet them. The simpleton never looks, and suffers the consequences.

He who gambles picks his own pocket...

Ecclesiastes 9:12

A man never knows when he is going to run into bad luck. He is like a fish caught in a net, or a bird caught in a snare.

144

He who sits down cannot make footprints in the sands of time...

Proverbs 12:24

Work hard and become a leader; be lazy and never succeed.

He who does one fault at first, and lies to hide it, makes it two—Watts...

Proverbs 26:18,19

A man who is caught lying to his neighbor and says, "I was just fooling," is like a madman throwing around firebrands, arrows and death.

He who kills time buries opportunities...

Proverbs 12:11

The wise man looks ahead. The fool attempts to fool himself and won't face facts.

He who has health has hope, and he who has hope has everything...

Psalm 146:5-6

But happy is the man who has the God of Jacob as his helper, whose hope is in the Lord his God—the God who made both earth and heaven, the seas and everything in them. He is the God who keeps every promise.

He who lies down with the dogs will get up with the fleas...

Proverbs 13:20

Be with wise men and become wise. Be with evil men and become evil.

He who marries for wealth sells his own liberty...

Proverbs 21:4,6

Pride, lust, and evil actions are all sin. Dishonest gain will never last, so why take the risk.

He who rises late must trot all day, and shall scarce overtake his business at night...

Proverbs 28:19

Hard work brings prosperity; playing around brings poverty.

He who tries to do something and fails is infinitely
better than he who tries to
do nothing and succeeds...

Proverbs 21:21

The man who tries to be good, loving, and
kind finds life, righteousness, and honor.

He who gets to the end of the rope should tie a knot and hang on...

Proverbs 18:14, 21:15

A man's courage can sustain his broken body, but when courage dies what hope is left? A good man loves justice, but it is a calamity to evil-doers.

153

He who is too busy for God is too busy...

Proverbs 29:18

When there is ignorance of God, the people run wild; but what a wonderful thing it is for a nation to know and keep his laws!

He who is wrapped up in himself is a very small package...

Proverbs 12:20

He who keeps [holds] malice harbors a viper in his heart.

He who exercises forethought spares afterthought...

Proverbs 19:2,3

It is dangerous and sinful to rush into the unknown. A man may ruin his chances by his own foolishness and then blame it on the Lord.

He who kneels to pray will not stumble...

Proverbs 3:6

In everything you do, put God first, and he will direct you and crown your efforts with success.

157

He who borrows often sorrows...

Proverbs 22:7

Just as the rich rule the poor, so the borrower is servant to the lender.

proverbs for people

*Terrify your ills and banish your blues
with Vernon McLellan's latest dose of
witty, provocative insights.*

Proverbs for Princes!
Proverbs for Paupers!
Proverbs for Everyone!

*The author of Quips, Quotes, and Quests
has done it again in this delightfully tantalizing
potpourri of penetrating insights and poignant
points that will add new dimensions to your life!*

---**ABOUT THE AUTHOR**---

Well-known author, recording artist,
and broadcaster Vernon McLellan is also the Vice-President
of International Programming for the PTL Television Network,
and has shared his contagious warmth, wit, and humor
with people around the world in scores of speaking
and concert appearances.

HARVEST HOUSE PUBLISHERS
Eugene, Oregon 97402

0-89081-326

Silhouette ❦ Romance

57255-5
$1.95

#255

JOAN
SMITH
Caprice